The Skill of Persuasion:

Simple ways to get others to cooperate with you

By

Alan R. Graham

Table of Content

Introduction

There has never been a better time for businessmen to master the art of persuasion than right now. The days of executives using command and control and managing by decree are long gone. Businesses nowadays are mainly administered by cross-functional teams of peers, with baby boomers and their Generation X progeny as the majority of employees. These generations have limited patience for unquestioning leadership. The old hierarchy has been further undermined by electronic communication and globalization as information and people move more freely than ever within organizations and choices are made closer to the marketplace. It basically comes down to this: work today is done in a setting where people don't merely ask "What should I do?" These fundamental changes that have been in the works for more than a decade but are now firmly established in the economic landscape, are the result of this. why should I do it, though?

Persuasion is necessary to adequately respond to this why question. However, a lot of businesspeople misuse persuasion, and even more underuse it. The cause? Most people think of persuasion as a technique used to close deals and sell items. It is also frequently perceived as being dishonest and to be avoided, just like other forms of manipulation. Persuasion can be used to close deals and close sales, but it can also be abused to control others. However, when used effectively and to its full extent, persuasion triumphs over sales and is in stark contrast to deception. An effective persuader guides colleagues to a problem's shared solution through a negotiation and learning process. To persuade someone to change their mind, they must be moved from their current viewpoint, but not by pleading or coercion. It requires careful planning, appropriate argument framing, the presentation of compelling data, and an effort to discover the right emotional fit with your audience.

Chapter 1

Dealing with Individuals

Have you ever been annoyed or frustrated by a tough or inept person? What if the other person is acting in a way that prevents them from doing what you want them to do for a reason or purpose that you are not yet aware of? We can obtain fresh knowledge that will enable us to modify our behavior for even better results when we take a few minutes to step outside of ourselves and observe the scenario from a different perspective.

I recently spoke with a coaching client who serves as the CEO of a significant business. He was annoyed because several of the modifications he suggested were being rejected by his chief operational officer. He realized how the COO might be feeling and why he reacted the way he did after pausing for a moment to view the issue from a different angle. He was able to communicate even more eloquently and compassionately as a result of these fresh perspectives, which improved the rapport, decreased resistance, and increased harmony among the senior leadership team members. Gaining a new viewpoint enables you to think more clearly, be more empathic, access new options, and make more objective decisions in many situations, especially during times of conflict or in other emotionally charged events.

In general, what we take to be reality is just what we take to be real. Before we even become aware of it, we filter our views depending on our prior experiences, values, beliefs, and expectations. This implies that different people may view a situation's truth or what is "right" differently. Although we may occasionally feel annoyed or provoked by someone in our lives, the underlying issue is frequently not that person but rather how we view them. When we alter our perspective, we may alter our actions and, consequently, our outcomes.

"Perceptual positions" is a potent method to assist you in doing this. With the help of this NLP tool, you can examine each encounter from three different angles. Your vision of the scenario might change once you've encountered all three of these points of view, and you might acquire crucial lessons that will make you feel more comfortable and enable you to react even more skillfully in the future.

The three perceptual positions are as follows:

1. Your perspective, or what NLP refers to as the "first position"
2. The perspective of the opposite party (sometimes known as the "second position").
3. An objective observer's perspective, or "third position"

Being able to shift between the various positions enables you to see a problem from all three perspectives before returning to yourself to choose the highest and best course of action.

Here is a drill to help you practice using this effective tool:

1. Think for a moment about a person who sets off your triggers or with whom you struggle to get along. Take into account how you feel about this individual, the circumstances, and what you believe to be true.

2. Visualise leaving your body, distancing yourself from your identity and feelings, and entering the body of the other person. Moving to the spot where the other person would be standing or sitting if they were with you right now can be done by physically leaving the original position. Be sure to adopt the other person's posture, attitudes, gestures, and other characteristics as you imagine yourself in their position. You will gain access to important information about what the other person may be hearing, seeing, thinking, and feeling that you might not otherwise have.

3. Reverse your gaze to the starting location and visualize yourself there. Take note of your perceptions about the person occupying the first place. You might sense emotions or have an instinctive hunch.

4. Now visualize yourself leaving the other person's body and moving to the third position, which is equivalent to the third

point of a triangle, where you can see both people. Be unbiased, like a fly on the wall watching both sides of the encounter with curiosity. What do you notice about the people in the first and second positions from this unbiased viewpoint? What guidance do you have for the first-place candidate?

5. Leave the third place and return to the starting position. Think about the current differences. Take note of your feelings regarding both the circumstance and the other person. What steps, if any, can you take to improve your outcomes the next time a similar circumstance arises?

The perceptual positions technique gives you the chance to view challenging circumstances or individuals in your life through a more objective lens. When you look at the big picture, you may uncover details that you may have previously erased or misinterpreted when you were emotionally invested in the drama of the circumstance. This gives you access to crucial lessons on how to modify your behavior in the future for even better outcomes.

I implore you to apply this strategy to foresee potential interactions or situations, or to draw lessons from the past to develop fresh viewpoints and answers.

Chapter Two

Psychological ploys to instantly win people over

It can be difficult to explain why you like someone. Perhaps it's their silly smile, perhaps it's their incisive wit, perhaps it's just that they're fun to be around. You simply enjoy them.

Scientists have spent years attempting to identify the precise variables that compel one individual to choose another, but they are typically unsatisfied with replies like that.

Here are some fascinating findings. Continue reading for information that will help you build stronger relationships more quickly and give a new perspective to your present friendships.

1. Imitate the person you are with.

This tactic, also known as mirroring, involves gently imitating the actions of another person. Try to mimic the motions, facial expressions, and body language of the person you are speaking to.

Researchers from New York University first identified the "chameleon effect," or when people unintentionally imitate one another's behavior, in 1999. That mimicry makes anything appealing.

72 male and female participants were given an assignment to complete with a partner. While researchers recorded the encounters, the partners (who worked for the researchers) either imitated the other participant's behavior or didn't. The participants were asked to rate how much they loved their partners after the interaction.

Indeed, when their spouse imitated their behavior, individuals were more likely to claim that they liked their partner.

2. Spend more time with the folks you want to become friends with.

The mere-exposure effect states that people tend to like others who are acquainted with them.

Psychologists at the University of Pittsburgh had four women pretend to be students in a college psychology class as one illustration of this occurrence. Different women attended class on different occasions. Male students displayed a larger affinity for the woman they had seen more frequently in class when experimenters showed them images of the four women, even though they hadn't interacted with any of them.

3. Give others praise

The adjectives you use to describe other people will be linked to your personality by others. Spontaneous trait transference is the name for this occurrence.

Gretchen Rubin, the author of "The Happiness Project," asserts that "whatever you say about other people influences how people see you."

People will relate to you as sincere and nice if you characterize someone else in those terms. The opposite is also true: If you frequently criticize others behind their backs, your friends will begin to think the same thing about you.

4. Attempt to exhibit optimistic feelings.

The term "emotional contagion" refers to the phenomenon whereby people are significantly impacted by the emotions of others. People can instinctively feel the emotions of those around them, according to a study from Ohio University and the University of Hawaii.

The authors of the study speculate that this may be because we frequently replicate the movements and expressions of others, which causes us to experience similar emotions.

Try your best to convey cheerful feelings to others if you want them to feel joyful around you.

5. Exude warmth and expertise

The stereotype content model, which postulates that people evaluate others based on their friendliness and competence, was developed by psychologists at Princeton University and their colleagues.

People will feel like they can trust you if you can project a warm, non-competitive, and friendly image of yourself, according to the model. They are more likely to respect you if you appear competent—for instance if you have high economic or educational status.

According to Harvard psychologist Amy Cuddy, it's crucial to show warmth before skill, especially in professional contexts.

According to Cuddy, it is essential to our survival from an evolutionary standpoint to determine whether a person earns our trust.

6. Periodically disclose your shortcomings.

The pratfall effect states that when you make a mistake, people will like you more – but only when they think you are a competent person. You become more relatable and vulnerable to those around you when you admit your flaws.

This phenomenon was first identified by University of Texas at Austin researcher Elliot Aronson while researching how inadvertent errors might change how attractive someone is considered. He requested that University of Minnesota male students listen to recordings of people taking a test.

The students gave those who performed well on the quiz but spilled coffee after the interview a higher likability rating than those who performed poorly on the quiz or did not perform well on the quiz and spilled coffee.

7. Highlight common values

A famous research by Theodore Newcomb found that people are more drawn to others who are like them. The similarity-attraction effect is what's behind this. In his study, Newcomb assessed the opinions of his participants towards touchy themes like politics and sex before placing them in a residence owned by the University of Michigan to live together.

When their housemates exhibited comparable attitudes about the topics studied towards the end of their stay, the subjects grew to like them more.

It's interesting to note that a more recent study by scientists at the University of Virginia and Washington University in St. Louis discovered that recruits to the Air Force liked each other more when they shared negative personality traits than when they did favorable ones.

8. Smile

In a University of Wyoming study, over 100 undergraduate women viewed photographs of another woman in one of four poses: smiling with the mouth open, smiling with the mouth closed, not smiling with the mouth open, or not smiling with the mouth closed. No matter where she was positioned in the picture, the woman appeared to be most appreciated when she was grinning.

More recently, researchers at Stanford University and the University of Duisburg-Essen discovered that when an avatar smiled more, students who engaged with each other via avatars felt better about the interaction.

According to a different study, smiling when you first meet someone increases the likelihood that they'll remember you afterward.

9. Consider the other person's point of view.

People desire to be seen in a way that supports the ideas they have about who they are. The self-verification theory can be used to explain this phenomenon. Whether our ideas are positive or negative, we all look for confirmation.

Participants with favorable and negative opinions of themselves were asked if they wished to interact with persons who had positive or negative opinions of them for a series of research at Stanford University and the University of Arizona.

Participants who had favorable self-views preferred compliments from others, while participants who had negative self-views chose criticism. This might be the case because people prefer to communicate with those whose input is compatible with their established identities.

According to other studies, we get along better with people when their opinions of us mirror our own. We feel understood, which is a crucial element of closeness, therefore that's probably why.

10. Let them in on a secret.

One of the strongest relationship-building strategies can be self-disclosure.

College students were divided into pairs and instructed to spend 45 minutes getting to know one another as part of a study conducted by academics at the State University of New York at Stony Brook, the California Graduate School of Family Psychology, the University of California, Santa Cruz, and Arizona State University.

Some student pairings were given a set of more probing and intimate questions by the experimenters. For instance, "How do you feel about your relationship with your mother?" was one of the intermediate questions. Other pairs were given questions meant for small conversations. One inquiry, for instance, asked, "What is your favorite holiday? Why?"

The students who had asked progressively intimate questions during the trial felt significantly more connected to one another than the students who had only made casual talk.

As you grow to know someone, you can use this method independently. For instance, you can progress from simple inquiries (such as what movie they just saw) to finding out about the people in their lives that matter the most to them. Someone is more likely to feel closer to you and want to confide in you in the future if you share sensitive information with them.

11. Demonstrate your ability to maintain their privacy.

According to two studies conducted by scientists at the University of Florida, Arizona State University, and Singapore Management University, people place a high value on relationships that are both trustworthy and trustworthy.

These two characteristics turned out to be very significant when participants were visualizing their ideal friend and coworker.

According to Suzanne Degges-White from Northern Illinois University, "Trustworthiness is comprised of several components, including honesty, dependability, and loyalty, and while each is important to successful relationships, honesty, and dependability has been identified as the most vital in the realm of friendships."

12. Demonstrate a sense of humor.

A sense of humor was crucial, according to research from Illinois State University and California State University at Los Angeles, whether respondents were envisioning their perfect friend or romantic relationship.

Another study from Illinois State University and DePaul University indicated that employing humor when getting to know someone can increase their liking of you. The research found that engaging in a humorous activity—for instance, teaching someone to dance while wearing a blindfold—can boost romantic attraction.

13. Allow them to introduce themselves.

Recently, Harvard researchers found that similar to food, money, and sex, talking about yourself may be intrinsically satisfying.

In one study, participants were asked to answer questions regarding either their own or another person's opinions while seated in an fMRI machine. A friend or family member waiting outside the fMRI machine had been requested to attend the study with the participant. Participants were sometimes informed that their answers would be shared with a friend or relative, while other times they would be kept secret.

The findings indicated that individuals' motivation and reward-related brain regions were most active while sharing knowledge with others, but they were also engaged when talking to themselves in private.

In other words, if you let someone talk about their life instead of droning on about yours, they might remember you more favorably.

14. Show some vulnerability

Jim Taylor from the University of San Francisco claims in an article on PsychologyToday.com that emotional openness, or lack thereof, can explain whether two people click or not.

Despite this, Taylor acknowledges that "emotional openness, of course, comes with risks that involve making yourself vulnerable and not knowing whether this emotional exposure will be accepted and reciprocated or rejected and deflected."

The same Illinois State University and California State University in Los Angeles study mentioned above revealed that expressiveness and openness are crucial and desirable qualities in ideal companions, so it might be worth the risk.

It doesn't matter if that companion is a friend or a romantic one.

15. Pretend to like them

A phenomenon known as "reciprocity of liking" has been studied by psychologists for some time. It states that when we believe someone likes us, we also tend to like them.

For instance, participants were informed in a 1959 study published in Human Relations that particular participants in a group discussion would probably appreciate them. The experimenter randomly assigned these individuals to these groups.

Those who claimed to like them were the persons who the participants said they liked the most after the debate.

More recently, scientists from the Universities of Waterloo and Manitoba discovered that when we expect someone to accept us, we act friendlier towards them, boosting the likelihood that they would in fact like us. Therefore, even if you're unsure of how someone feels about you, act as though you do, and they'll probably respond the same way.

Making a Strong First Impression

When you meet someone for the first time, it only takes three seconds for them to form an opinion of you. The other person forms an opinion about you in this brief period based on your look, body language, demeanor, mannerisms, and how you are dressed.

Every time you interact with a new person, they assess you and create an opinion of you. These first impressions frequently set the manner for the relationship that follows and can be very difficult to change or undo.

Consequently, you must understand how to make an amazing first impression. To enable you do this, this article offers some helpful advice

Steps on Making a Great First Impression

1. Be punctual

Your "good excuse" for being late won't fascinate someone you are meeting for the first time. Plan to arrive a few minutes early and leave yourself some leeway in case of traffic delays or making a mistake turn. Arriving on time is the first step in making a strong first impression and is much preferable to arriving late.

Check your tech and connection in advance if your first encounter is virtual, and consider your surroundings and backdrop.

2. Display Yourself Respectfully

Of course, the look is important. When you meet someone for the first time, they don't know you, therefore the first thing they notice about you your looks.

But don't be alarmed! This does not imply that you must be flawless to make a powerful and favorable first impression.

(Except, of course, if you are interviewing with your neighborhood modeling agency.). Making a good impression is all about how you present yourself.

Since a picture is worth a thousand words, the "picture" you first give to a new acquaintance must reflect who you are.

First, consider your clothing choices. What kind of attire is appropriate for the meeting or situation? What kind of clothing should you wear in a professional setting? Suit, blazer, or casual attire? What sort of clothing is the person you're meeting likely to be wearing? A pinstripe business suit might not be the best choice if your contact works in the performing or visual arts.

When in a foreign environment or country, you should pay particular attention to the suitable attire for business and social encounters because it differs between cultures. Ensure that you are familiar with the customs and traditions of the nation and culture you are meeting in.

3. Be Who You Are

Yes, you do need to "fit in" a little bit if you want to make a good impression. However, it does not include becoming someone you are not or losing who you are. Being yourself is the best approach to making an impact. You'll feel more confident, be able to establish trust and gain the respect and integrity of the people you encounter if you do this.

4. Display a Glorious Smile!

As they say, "Smile and the world smiles too." So nothing makes a good first impression like a smile. A kind smile that exudes confidence will put the other person at ease. So when it comes to making a good first impression, smiling wins. But be careful not to exaggerate it; those who do so risk coming across as smarmy and insincere.

5. Be frank and assured

It's often true that body language conveys more information than words when it comes to generating a strong first impression.

Use your body language to epress the right amount of assurance and confidence. Make eye contact, stand tall, smile (of course), and extend a solid handshake in greeting. All of this will support your confidence-projecting efforts and help you and the other person feel more comfortable.

When meeting someone for the first time, almost everyone experiences some degree of nervousness. However, this could result in undesirable side effects including sweaty hands, the "jitters," or nail biting. You can try to control your nervous tendencies by becoming aware of them.

6. Make Petite Talk

On the verbal give and take, conversations are built. Asking the individual you are meeting some questions in advance could be helpful. Alternatively, spend a few minutes getting to know them. Do they, for instance, play golf? Do they collaborate with a nearby nonprofit organization? Do you have any similarities with them? If so, doing so can be a terrific way to start and maintain a conversation.

7. Be optimistic.

All of your actions exhibit a positive mindset. So, even when feeling nervous or facing criticism, present an optimistic attitude. Make an effort to absorb meeting information and provide useful input. Finally, keep your attitude upbeat and smile to convey that you are approachable.

8. Show respect and pay attention.

Having good manners and acting in an attentive, polite, and courteous manner aid in creating a positive first impression.

 If you do anything less, it could sabotage your one chance to make a good first impression. Do your best to behave, then!

To offer the person your whole attention, put aside modern distractions, such as turning off your mobile phone. Likewise, avoid being distracted by others. After all, if you are more interested in chatting with someone else, what kind of first impression would you make? Your full focus should be given to your new acquaintance. Anything less will probably cause them to feel disregarded or even irritated.

How to Increase Attraction

Do you have any appeal? If not, don't worry—there are approaches to raising your level of interest. It can significantly impact your life and is easier than you might imagine. The key to being intriguing is to be genuinely curious and enthusiastic about life. Being more fascinating is a definite method to improve your social life, whether you want to meet new friends, impress your boss, or find a romantic partner.

Be Curious and Ask a Lot of Questions:

Being genuinely curious about the world around you is one of the best ways to stand out. You're more likely to converse and ask inquiries when you're intrigued. Additionally, you'll be more receptive to new things. Social psychologists have discovered that folks who are inquisitive and frequently ask questions are frequently seen as more likable than those who are not.

Don't only ask questions, though—collect facts on your own as well—to be truly intriguing. You will become more knowledgeable as a result, and people will be in awe of your skills.

Be receptive to new encounters and encountering new people.

Being open to new experiences is crucial if you want to be more intriguing. This includes socializing with strangers. Make an effort to get to know new people and their interests when you meet them.

Even if you don't know someone well, make an effort to engage them in conversation. For instance, if you're at a party, try to engage with a variety of people. You'll not only become more intriguing as a result, but you'll also be more likely to make new friends and find romantic partners.

Be a Good Storyteller

An interesting person is often a good storyteller. When you share your experiences with others, make sure to make them intriguing. This does not mean that you should make up stories; just be sure to focus on the most interesting aspects of your life.

If you can make your stories entertaining, people will be more likely to remember you—and they'll also be more interested in hearing more from you in the future.

Talk About Things That Appeal You Even If They Are Not Mainstream

If you're emotional about something, don't be afraid to talk about it—even if it's not mainstream. When you're excited about a topic, it's more likely to come across as interesting. This is because people are attracted to others who are passionate about something.

So, if you're a fan of a certain band or TV program, don't be shy about telling others about it. You never know; you might make a new acquaintance who is into the same things that you are.

Accept who you are, flaws and all

Avoid attempting to be someone you are not since it will likely come across as artificial and boring. Instead, celebrate your individuality and let your actual self emerge. Don't be frightened to be yourself since people are drawn to individuals who are sincere and true.

Honestly and Openly Share Your Thoughts and Opinions

It's crucial to express your ideas honestly and openly if you want to come off as more fascinating. This doesn't imply that you must express your views on every subject; only make sure to do so when requested.

Even if they disagree with you, people will appreciate you for being honest about your beliefs.

Pay Attention to Details That Tell a Story about You

Everything you do, from what you wear to your hair and makeup routine to the jewelry you wear, communicates something about who you are. Pay attention to the aspects about yourself that convey a story if you want to be intriguing.

Enjoy yourself and avoid taking yourself too seriously.

Having fun and don't take yourself too seriously is one of the finest strategies to be more fascinating. Other people are more inclined to find something fascinating while you are having fun. This is because people are drawn to those that are positive and enjoyable.

Chapter 3

Persuading others to adopt your viewpoint

Not everyone will share your opinions on everything. That is what makes this universe so fascinating and diverse. We all have our distinctive perspectives on the world, and we've all had various experiences that have shaped us in various ways.

Some situations require you to persuade individuals you have stewardship over to agree with you, such as when you're the company president or a parent who wants their children to understand why they're leaving the place they love.

Here are some pointers to assist you gradually tip the scales in your favor.

1. Respect other people's opinions

Since no two persons are the same, there will inevitably be disparities in viewpoint. But as a leader, you cannot tell someone outright that they are mistaken. The individual's IQ, judgment, pride, and self-respect will all take a direct hit as a result. Additionally, it is only natural to detest the individual who abruptly ends your sentence. This means the person will just harden his heart against you and grow more certain of his beliefs. So, sincerely attempt to understand the situation from that person's perspective. It will make it easier for you to comprehend their perspective and the reasons for their beliefs. This can also help you understand how to respond to their worries and inquiries. Additionally, it demonstrates your sensitivity and regard for them, which will help you make a positive impression.

2. Keep in mind that you can't win a debate.

The word "argument" has both positive and bad connotations; while it encourages both sides to discuss their points of view and ideas, it also sets off a flurry of emotions that typically result in no one winning. So think about your eventual aim before a conversation devolves into an argument. It will almost always be something that cannot be resolved by discussion. So take a big breath, keep in mind the desired outcome, and talk without getting heated, insulting, or confrontational.

3. Admit when you're incorrect.

Accepting that we cannot always be correct is not shameful; on the contrary, it demonstrates leadership humility. If you believe you have erred, swiftly and diplomatically admit it to the other person and express your want to make it right.

It not only demonstrates your willingness to take the lead but also your practicality, drive to succeed, and capacity for being realistic when necessary.

4. Focus on areas of agreement

Developing a connection with the other person around shared interests can serve as a good place to start. An affirmative response has a psychological effect, and this is a well-known strategy utilized by solicitors in court. If you say "yes," the other person is likely to agree with you more. You can take advantage of this by simply being more amiable. Do not, however, lie or consent to something in which you do not genuinely believe. Build on the rapport you've established with the other person through their affirmative responses and gradually persuade them to agree with you.

5. Allow them to think the concept is their own.

The secret to accomplishing this is to communicate your concept in such a subtly elegant way that the other person builds on it and even begins to believe that they came up with it. Although it could be difficult to let someone else take credit for your concept, they will be happy to carry it out and even be pleased about it, which is exactly what you wanted. The active support you will receive from their end is yet another benefit.

6. Make use of the higher purposes

Everyone has an idealistic nature, therefore appealing to such feelings might influence how someone sees you. Honesty, truthfulness, readiness, and sincerity are only a few examples of noble impulses. At the end of the day, we all want to choose the correct course, and a gentle reminder works well to persuade others to feel the same way.

How to Persuade Others to Work with You

Symphonies are impossible to whistle. It needs an entire orchestra to accomplish it. H. E. Luccock

No man or woman is an island, regardless of how autonomous we may think we are. At home, at business, and in our daily encounters, cooperation is essential. If your experience has been anything like mine, you may find that frustrating at times. It may seem as though other people are being obstructionist, don't want to work with you, or don't share your values.

What distinguishes "cooperation" from "teamwork," you may wonder? Teamwork is the collaborative effort of a group of people to achieve a common goal, whereas cooperation is the act of cooperating. For instance, you are cooperating if you agree to hold my umbrella while I look for my phone in my handbag while I'm waiting for a bus in the rain. Teamwork would be demonstrated if those of us at the bus stop decided to push the broken-down bus in the hopes that it would start. We are not all on the same team, so I have opted to concentrate on encouraging cooperation because we always need the cooperation of others.

What is your process then? Well, telling others to comply with you just isn't effective, and neither is making assumptions. You must Ask, Listen, and Facilitate to encourage cooperation. Here's how:

Ask with Clarity

If others don't know exactly what they should be doing, they might not comply with you; too frequently, our "Ask" isn't clear. Perfecting your ask and having the guts to make it are two topics covered in one of the first courses of my online program.

Are the actions you want the individual you want to work with you to take clear to them? How will they be able to tell if they are succeeding? Have you conveyed your grand vision to motivate them to take action?

Because they can't read my mind, I've learned that when my request isn't clear, I end up believing that people aren't cooperating with me.

Good communication and cooperation go hand in hand. Make sure you are not basing your decisions on assumptions, and consider using a psychometric test to better understand both your own and other people's communication preferences.

Aim for Inspiration

It's critical to comprehend someone's motivations if you wish to encourage cooperation with them. Don't assume that what motivates you will also motivate others.

Pay attention to hints as to what motivates them. If you're having trouble with this, try explaining all the different ways they'll gain by cooperation. They might be able to solve a problem, save time or money, accomplish a goal, discover something new, or obtain recognition as a result. By doing this, you are appealing to their motivation and demonstrating why they would want to work with you.

Make sure they understand how important their activities are.

Contribute to the How

You must make sure they have the means to work with you in addition to asking and listening. After all, they might just lack the necessary knowledge or resources. Do they require coaching, mentoring, or training? Have you gone through each stage in sufficient detail and at the appropriate level for them? Even though you may have already conveyed everything to them, they might still require a recap.

In conclusion, be sure to approach encouraging cooperation with respect, decency, and transparency.

Chapter 4

Being a leader

How Do You Become a Leader? What Does a Leader Do?

Who comes to your mind when you think about great leaders?

One can think of influential individuals like Winston Churchill and Nelson Mandela, or possibly Mahatma Gandhi and Martin Luther King Jr.

But determining what distinguishes these historical figures as good leaders turns out to be more difficult. Was it more than just their position that made them persuasive leaders?

Even though we have all had leadership roles in our lives, we are rarely asked to explain "what is a good leader." The answers differ from organization to organization and person to person, making it extremely hard to pin down the characteristics of leadership.

Do you have any thoughts on your career's future move? This essay examines what leadership is, what it entails, how it differs from management, and how to improve as a leader.

What is a leader?

The following are straightforward analyses of the query, "What is a leader?"

1. A leader is an individual who gives people a sense of purpose and inspiration.
2. A leader is an individual who has a vision and knows how to get there.
3. A leader is someone who provides their team with the resources and encouragement they need to succeed.

A leader could be either of those, but a thriving leader possesses all three qualities.

An effective leader knows what it will take to accomplish their team's objectives and has a common vision that is in line with their fundamental beliefs. They lead, manage, and encourage their teams to work imaginatively and self-assuredly toward that common goal.

A leader gives their team members the tools they need to embrace their leadership traits and act with passion and independence. Additionally, they encourage and motivate their employees to continue making long-term progress and show enthusiasm for reaching their objectives.

What is a leader's function?

Now that you are aware of what a leader is, you might still wonder: "What does a leader do?" In this case, the determined response "it depends" is largely applicable. Depending on the size of their group, organization, or base, each leader's precise responsibilities vary. Additionally, it depends on their ideals and objectives, both immediate and long-term.

A leader's primary commitments include coaching, directing, and inspiring people. They lead individuals through career advancements and inspire teams through difficult times. To keep teams aligned and working towards common objectives, a leader effectively manages people. They encourage teamwork and set an example for others.

A leader's duties are what?

As you can see, a leader is charged with several tasks. However, they frequently fit into one of three categories:

- Coach
- Inspire
- Guide

Coach

A good leader uses coaching and mentoring to assist their team members and employees grow. Asynchronous touch points and one-on-one encounters are two possible ways to do this. And the majority of their coaching works its way up to helping the company's overarching objectives.

A great leader will strike a balance between the objectives of the organization and the employees, making the growth of every individual a mutually beneficial connection. The development of the individual frequently parallels that of the business.

Guide

Leaders do not only coach but also mentor their team members. This is accomplished through creating and managing teams, establishing objectives, coming up with plans for achieving those objectives and guiding workers through the process.

A leader can help their team members, for instance, through unpleasant dialogues or different approaches to problem-solving.

Inspire

To inspire is one underrated leadership responsibility. A strong leader may motivate their team members and important stakeholders by using their storytelling, empathy, and communication abilities.

A leader's responsibility includes motivating others, whether it involves supporting a direct report's promotion, objecting to a strategy, or managing a team that has fallen short of its targets.

Characteristic traits of a leader

Despite their audacity, leaders never abandon their teams. Leaders embrace a variety of leadership attributes and can't be reduced to a single style since they must strike a balance between vision and support that enables team members to accomplish agreed goals.

Leaders in general frequently have these seven key traits:

Purpose: It's challenging to inspire team members in the absence of a sense of purpose. People are empowered by leaders to understand the motivation behind particular goals, allowing them to participate equally. Making daily operations feel more purposeful contributes to preserving team motivation and individual commitment to bigger objectives. Individual accountability is encouraged in teams by leaders who integrate a sense of personal purpose into the overarching mission of the organization. This inspires team members to embrace their personal leadership skills to attain larger goals.

Motivation: Creating goals that are connected with values helps leaders inspire their teams to work towards the organization's vision. Leaders enable their team members to work arduously beyond their responsibilities towards a common objective by consistently reaching out to them. Motivation extends beyond motivational speeches. Talking and listening to their teams is a key component of great leadership. Giving instructions and manipulating outcomes are not the goals of leadership; rather, it is about listening, encouraging, and bringing out the best in people.

Vision: Leaders can unify their team behind their vision because they have a larger perspective. Leaders motivate their team with an end goal that resonates with individual values and motivates action by leveraging team strengths and core beliefs. Without a unified vision that is in line with fundamental principles, businesses frequently find themselves meeting targets without moving the business in the desired direction. Growth does not equate to surviving. Leaders have a vision for development and enlargement.

Empathy: Leaders have sympathy for the people in their team. It's how they motivate individuals to go above and beyond what's required of them to accomplish a common goal. Leaders instill a sense of value through listening and showing their admiration for their teams. Leaders can inspire teams to see the vision for themselves and take action to make it a reality when they prioritize empathy and recognize the contributions of their team members. Putting themselves in their team members' shoes also aids leaders in addressing important issues and offering solutions.

Creativity: Managers might be tempted to maintain the status quo, but leaders innovate in big, original ways. Instead of bothering about the chain of authority, leaders urge their staff to ask "Why?" and use innovative thinking to see the wider picture. Leaders embrace new ways of conceptualizing and strategizing because they are guided by a lofty vision. Nothing is off the table when it comes to offering creative and more successful approaches to pursue and succeed in long-term goals.

A Shared Vision: Although the company's management may set the broad direction, their vision will mean nothing if it doesn't resonate with the team. Leaders can weave their long-term objectives via individually inspiring and rewarding achievement by investigating the values and personal objectives that give team members purpose. Team members are motivated to go above and beyond their duties to achieve their goals when they share their leader's vision and beliefs.

Always trying to improve: Leaders never stop improving themselves. With an eye toward growth, leaders continuously seek opportunities to improve for themselves and their teams. This leaning towards personal improvement means leaders actively seek feedback and respect ideas that favor effectiveness and improvement over defending their egos. When leaders create an environment where feedback isn't just beneficial but highly valued, they inspire team members to voice their thoughts and bring the best ideas to the table. This can lead to higher innovation and long-term success.

How to Improve As a Leader

There is always room for improvement as a leader, and the precise stages you take will depend on your experience level, character traits, and objectives. But no matter where you are in your leadership development, you can improve as a leader by following these three stages.

Step 1: Listen and take notes:

Social abilities, not force and control, are what make a leader. The best leaders invest the necessary time in learning about their team members' leadership styles and taking the time to listen to them.

Give your team members the chance to take advantage of their abilities and work as efficiently as possible. Ask for opinions and find out what the staff members think. Team members will be more motivated to work passionately towards causes they care about and believe in if they feel personally valued.

Step 2: Establish team-wide objectives:

Leaders have a clear vision for the future and invest time in getting to know the aspirations and goals of their team members. This can make sure that everyone feels important and included in the organization's bigger mission.

Investigate the core values of your team members and incorporate them into more general, team- and organization-wide goals. By assisting your team members in finding greater purpose and fulfillment in their jobs, you'll inspire them to go above and beyond the call of duty to contribute to innovation.

Step 3: Continue to look for methods to get better.

Leaders are always looking for ways to improve both their teams and themselves.

Who do you admire as a leader? Who presently occupies the leadership position you can picture yourself in? Learn more about those leaders, and think about asking one of them to be your mentor.

Your coworkers and team members could also provide you with chances to grow. Create chances for open dialogue and feedback at all organizational levels.

When giving feedback to others, combine open communication with more tools so that team members can hone their abilities and play to their strengths. They will be able to respond to situations more creatively and provide their best effort in any circumstance as a result.

Conclusion

Being deeply invested in your project yourself is a certain method to pique others' interest in it and persuade them to join you. Genuine enthusiasm and fervor spread quickly, especially when their effects are obvious. Increasing your impact via leadership and conviction won't bring you millions of fans. However, it can have a more long-lasting rippling effect at work, influencing organizational decisions, culture, and direction while fostering devotion and loyalty. You might not be aware that the things you're doing are affecting other people as you gain influence. Because that's what you do and who you are, you might be thorough, provide feedback, encourage a colleague, or finish a difficult assignment. You grow as a person when no one is watching. You only realize you are actually explaining what it means to influence others in the afterthought.